Kenzie

D0560344

# Love & War

# Devotional for Couples

# JOHN & STASI ELDREDGE

Best-selling authors of *Wild at Heart* and *Captivating*

# Love & War

## Devotional
### *for* Couples

The 8-week adventure that will help you find
the marriage you always dreamed of

WATERBROOK
PRESS

LOVE AND WAR DEVOTIONAL FOR COUPLES
PUBLISHED BY WATERBROOK PRESS
12265 Oracle Boulevard, Suite 200
Colorado Springs, Colorado 80921

Hardcover ISBN 978-0-307-72993-4
eBook ISBN 978-0-307-72994-1

Library of Congress Cataloging-in-Publication Data
Eldredge, John, 1960–
    Love and war devotional for couples : the 8-week adventure that will help you find the marriage you always dreamed of / John and Stasi Eldredge.—1st ed.
        p. cm.
    ISBN 978-0-307-72993-4—ISBN 978-0-307-72994-1 (electronic)  1. Spouses—Prayers and devotions. 2. Marriage—Religious aspects—Christianity—Meditations. I. Eldredge, Stasi. II. Title.
    BV4596.M3E43 2011
    242'.644—dc22

                                2010027090

Printed in the United States of America
2016

10 9

SPECIAL SALES

# CONTENTS

# INTRODUCTION

Our lives are lived moment by moment, in increments we can actually handle. Our marriages are lived the same way. Not anniversary to anniversary or even month to month, but daily—in the ordinary ins and outs of time. The choices we make in the moments create the lives we enjoy—or don't. Thus, a love and war devotional. This devotional is a tool for you, for your marriage. We invite you to walk alongside us for eight weeks—five days a week—and dive deeper into the tangible realities of your marriage. We'll focus on Scripture and the heart of God and the heart that he placed in you and the heart he has placed in your spouse.

The journey of our lives is a journey of transformation. We are here to learn how to love. How do we learn? Moment by moment. Day by day. Week by week. Our marriages grow and become what God intended and what we ultimately long for in the same way. We are all of us learning to love.

Let's learn together.

# Remembering What We Wanted

# *Romance Meets Reality*

❧

*We love because he first loved us.*

—1 John 4:19

We probably ought to just start here: marriage is fabulously hard.

Maybe that's an odd way to begin, but it is *true,* and everybody who's been married knows this, though years into marriage it still catches us off guard, all of us. And newly married couples, when they discover how hard it is, seem genuinely surprised. Shocked and disheartened by the fact. *Are we doing something wrong? Did I marry the right person?* The wonders that lure us into marriage—romance, love, passion, sex, longing, companionship—sometimes seem so far from the actual reality of married life that we wind up fearing we've made a colossal mistake, caught the wrong bus, missed our flight. And so the hardness of marriage can also come as something of an embarrassment.

Or maybe it's just us. Don't you feel embarrassed to admit how hard your marriage is?

Yep. This is everyone. We might as well come out and admit it.

The sooner we get that shame off our backs, the sooner we'll find our way through. Of course marriage is hard. In fact, if you look back at the first marriage, that fairy-tale start in Genesis, you see that Adam and Eve had a pretty rough go at it. And they didn't even have parents to screw them up as children or friends giving them ridiculous advice. The fall of man seems to come during the honeymoon or shortly thereafter. (And how many honeymoon stories seem to reenact that little drama?) They hit rough water as soon as they set sail. This is the story of the first marriage, and it's a bit sobering.

But it also gives us some encouragement. It's normal for marriage to be hard. Even the best of marriages.

And God is in that.

In order to have the life we want, the life we are made for, and the marriage we long for, we need God. That's a very good thing! Because without him, nothing is as it should be. With him, all things are possible. Yes, marriage can be extremely hard. But that is not a reason to despair. Nor is it the final truth. There are seasons in marriage—in every relationship. Marriage is meant to be wonderful, and most of the time it is. Though it's sometimes so hard, think of the difficulty as a doorway. A doorway to all the *more* Jesus has for us in himself! There is hope!

*Dear God, as I begin this study, I offer up this time for your purposes. Please help me draw closer to your heart and deepen my marriage in every good way. Sometimes it is very hard. Even painful. I invite you into that as well. Have your way with me, with my spouse, and with our marriage. We need you. I am looking to you. In Jesus' mighty name, amen.*

Not only so, but we also rejoice in our sufferings, because we know that suffering produces perseverance; perseverance, character; and character, hope. And hope does not disappoint us, because God has poured out his love into our hearts by the Holy Spirit, whom he has given us. (Romans 5:3–5)

# DAY 2

# *Recovering Desire*

❧

*"What do you want?"—Jesus*

Somewhere along the way, we all lose heart in marriage. We all do. It happens to the best of us. The Dan Fogelberg song "Along the Road" speaks of a relationship that has "joy at the start," and suggests that along the journey, the heart "gets lost in the learning."

We might find a way to manage our disappointment. We might do our best to fight off resignation, but it works its way in. We let go of what we wanted, what we dreamed of, what we were created for. We begin to settle. Oftentimes we even forget what it was we wanted in the first place!

Because marriage is hard, sometimes painfully hard, your first great battle is not to lose heart. That begins with recovering desire—the desire for the love that is written on your heart. Let desire return. Let it remind you of all that you wanted, all that you were created for. And then consider this—what if God could bring you your heart's desire? What if the two of you could find your way to something beautiful?

That would be worth fighting for.

Don't start with, *How can that happen?* The *how* will come in time. You have to begin with *desire*. Start with what is written on your heart. What was it that you once dreamed of as a young man or woman? What was it you wanted when you fell in love?

*Father, thank you for my marriage. Thank you for my spouse. Lord, you know where we are with each other right now. You know the desires we each had coming into our marriage even if they were unclear to us. And only you know the dreams you have for our marriage. Once again, I give my marriage to you. I surrender myself, my spouse, and our life to you, and I ask for your will to be done in us and through us. Holy Spirit, blow gently onto the embers of our heart's desires where we have forgotten or abandoned what you placed there. Rekindle the flame. Remind us. And help us keep our eyes on you as the source of all that is good*

*and lovely and worth living for. Let hope rise. In Jesus'*
*name, amen.*

---

You open your hand and satisfy the desires
of every living thing. (Psalm 145:16)

# DAY 3

# *A Glorious Difficulty*

∽

*How good and pleasant it is when*
*brothers [and sisters] live together*
*in unity!*

—PSALM 133:1

Marriage is glorious. And yes, sometimes marriage is difficult. Okay. A lot of the time it is difficult. For everyone. This doesn't necessarily mean we are blowing it. Partly, it simply means we are human beings. When John and I got married, we looked forward to years of intimacy and laughter and the joy of being husband and wife. Our expectations of ease and marital bliss were quickly... not met. We were stunned. Most couples are. But, for heaven's sake, bringing together a man and a woman—two creatures who think, act, and feel so differently—and asking them to get along for the rest of their lives under the same roof is like taking Cinderella and

Huck Finn, tossing them in a submarine, and locking the hatch. What should we think will happen?

Actually, before you lock the hatch, toss in the constant experience of all our fears, our wounded hearts, our self-centeredness, our self-doubts, and our resolute commitments to self-protection. Good Lord, help us. Anyone looking for undeniable proof of the existence of God need look no further. The fact that *any* marriage makes it is a miracle of the first order. Bona fide proof that there are forces in the universe working on behalf of mankind.

Think of all those fairy tales about a boy and girl who find themselves thrown together in a dangerous land, working together while each carries a tragic flaw that pricks the other. Those fairy tales have it right. The husband is that boy. The wife is that girl. And your life is the adventure through that dangerous land.

But gloriously, we all are on the road to becoming the man or the woman we are meant to be. To cooperate with God and yield to his desires for our lives is what speeds the process. None of us is perfect. In fact, many of our unique quirks are not so endearing! Though we share much in common with our spouses, we are *so* different from each other as well. Wonderfully, *gloriously* different.

---

*Dear God, I surrender my life to you again today.*
*I want to be the person that you have created me to*
*be. Please show me the areas in my life that I need*

*to repent of and be healed of. I want to change for the good. I choose to cooperate with you. Lord, I pray to see my life and my marriage the way you do. I don't want to just eke by in our marriage. I want all the life and joy and victory and oneness that's possible! In your name, Jesus, I pray. Amen.*

---

I can do everything through Christ, who gives me strength. (Philippians 4:13, NLT)

# *The Centrality of Marriage*

*A new command I give you: Love one another.*

—JOHN 13:34

The Bible begins with a marriage and ends with a marriage. From start to finish, the part of this great story we have been given to play begins and ends with a marriage. Holy cow! What have we been missing here? Why does God give marriage such a central part in this story of redemption? What does he know that we don't yet see?

Well, let's begin here—this is a love story.

God is love, the apostle John tells us, and then he says it again so that we don't forget: "God is love, and the one who abides in love abides in God" (1 John 4:16, NASB). Love is the single most defining quality of his character and his life. God is a passionate and jealous lover (is there really any other kind?). Out of his love, he creates us for love. "We love because he first loved us" (1 John 4:19).

The Scriptures tell us we are made in God's image, and you'll notice that we human beings are, above all else, deeply and profoundly *relational*. All because he is. God is Trinity, a fellowship of love. Love and intimacy are the core of his being, and so he gives to each of us a heart like his. In doing this, God reveals our deepest purpose—to love and be loved.

This is a love story. And love is the deepest yearning of our hearts.

---

*Dear Lord, I'm beginning to remember that love is central to the story you are telling. Love is central to everything. Yes, I want to be loved. And I want to be a loving person. Thank you for loving me. Endlessly. Perfectly. Marvelously. I pray to marinate in your love for me. Open my eyes today to see even more clearly how much you love me, and then, God, let your love flow through me. In Jesus' name I pray, amen.*

---

Then I saw a new heaven and a new earth....
I saw the Holy City, the new Jerusalem, coming
down out of heaven from God, prepared as a
bride beautifully dressed for her husband....
Come, I will show you the bride, the wife of the
Lamb. (Revelation 21:1–2, 9)

DAY 5

# The Larger Story

*Then [Jesus] told them many things*
*in parables.*

—Matthew 13:3

God created marriage as a living, breathing portrait laid out before the eyes of the world so that all might see the story of the ages. A love story, set in the midst of desperate times. It is a story of redemption, a story of healing; it is a story of love. God gives us marriage to illustrate his heart for us. It is the deepest and most mythic reality in the world—that love is true and that God pursues us.

Our love is meant to be a picture of both his love and his fight. The masculine and the feminine, the courage and sacrifice, and yes, the beauty and the blood, sweat, and tears—these play out for us, and for the world, the story of the truest Love and his Beloved. God is fighting for the hearts of his people. He is a valiant king, a lover, who will set his people free.

Your marriage is part of a larger story, a story as romantic as any that's ever stirred your heart, and at least as dangerous. Why is it dangerous? Because love is always a risk. The sooner you come to terms with this fact, the sooner you can understand what is happening in your marriage. We cheer the hero and the heroine on because we can see what's at stake—the kingdom depends on their success. But we haven't anything close to this sort of perfect clarity in our marriages; we'd be hard pressed to name one simple thing that hangs in the balance (apart from our sanity and our grandmother's silver).

I'll wager that 90 percent of the confusion, misunderstanding, struggle, and disappointment in marriage is due to the fact that we do not understand what God is up to.

God is a great lover, and he created marriage to play out a daily living, breathing portrait of the intimacy he longs for with his people. *Gulp.* This is why it has such a central role. It is a kind of incarnation, *a passion play* about the love and union between Jesus and his beloved. Which might help you appreciate why the fury of hell has been unleashed against it.

---

*Dear Jesus, unveil for us the importance not only of marriage but of our marriage—to you and to your kingdom. I love that you are a valiant king who came to set his people free and who comes still. I give you our marriage and pray that it becomes ever increasingly a*

*picture to the world of the love story you are telling.*
*Protect my marriage. You are a warrior king. I pray*
*that you will fight for us and all you have for us. I will*
*join you. In Jesus' name, amen.*

---

Beloved, let us love one another.
(1 John 4:7, NASB)

## EXERCISE

What scenes from favorite movies or books have captured your heart over the years? It is good to remember. Linger with that question, and ask God what it is about those stories that drew you to them. What songs, what stories, what moments have awakened the deep desires of your heart? Does your spouse know your favorites? Do you know your spouse's? Why don't you ask? What does this tell you about your hearts?

# The Two Shall Become One

# DAY 1

# *The High Calling of Marriage*

∽

*Love never fails.*

—1 CORINTHIANS 13:8

We are urged to love, commanded to love, warned to love, implored to love. With abandon. Over and over and over again.

And what we want to ask is, *for goodness' sake, why?*

Maybe because of what is at stake.

In marriage, we are entrusted with the heart of another human being. Whatever else our life's great mission will entail, loving and defending the heart next to ours is part of our great quest.

Marriage is the privilege and the honor of living as close to the heart as two people can get. No one else in all the world has the opportunity to know each other more intimately than do a husband

and wife. We are invited into our spouses' secret lives, their truest selves; we come to know their nuances, their particular tastes, what they think is funny, what drives them crazy. We are entrusted with our spouses' hopes and dreams, their wounds, their fears.

An incredible honor is bestowed on the one to whom we pledge our lives, and a deep privilege is given to us as well. Not only is marriage good for a person (according to studies, it adds an average of seven years to the life of a man and three to a woman's life), married people as a whole say their lives are happier than those who are single report. Married people are healthier and better off financially. And the impact of a lasting marriage on the couple's children is sobering. Children of divorce do not fare nearly so well in life as those who grew up in an intact family.

Without you, your spouse will not become the man or the woman that God intends and the kingdom of God will not advance as it is meant to advance. Your spouse plays the most vital role in your life. You play the most critical role in your spouse's. No one will have a greater impact on your spouse's soul than you. No one has greater access to your spouse's heart than you. *This is an enormous honor.*

Marriage is the sanctuary of the heart.

---

*Dear Jesus, thank you for giving me my spouse. Thank you for entrusting me with that heart! Oh God, please*

*give me your vision for this person and help me to*
*love my spouse into that! I pray that our marriage*
*would be a safe place, a sanctuary from the world.*
*I pray you would increase in us the desire to offer rest*
*to each other. I pray we will experience sanctuary more*
*from each other. In your name I pray, amen.*

---

Be very careful, then, how you live—not as
unwise but as wise, making the most of every
opportunity.... Submit to one another out of
reverence for Christ. (Ephesians 5:15–16, 21)

# The Cost of Marriage

*If God is for us, who can be against us? He who
did not spare his own Son, but gave him up for
us all—how will he not also, along with him,
graciously give us all things?*

—ROMANS 8:31–32

Being married costs you everything. Not to mention tears, sleepless nights, incredible vulnerability, and countless sacrifices. It causes you to take a deeper look inside your heart and soul, your desires and your personality. It hurts, and it is not easy.

But, of course, you already know that.

It's no surprise that loving costs everything—look at the Cross. The good news is, loving is always worth it. We all know that loving is hard. Marriage is hard. But it is hard because it is so valuable that it is *opposed*. The devil hates marriage; he hates the beautiful picture of Jesus and his Bride that it represents. He hates love and life and beauty in all its forms. The world hates marriage. It hates unity and faithfulness and monogamy. Our flesh is not our ally here either; it rebels when we put others before ourselves. Our flesh hates dying!

But God loves marriage. The Holy Trinity is completely for it. God loves intimacy, friendship, unity, self-sacrifice, laughter, pleasure, joy, and the picture of the sacred romance you have the opportunity to present to the watching world. God is with you. He is for you. He commands you to love, and he says that with him, and in him, all things are possible.

Not easy. But not impossible. *Possible.*

Marriage is going to ask everything of you, and that is why you must have a vision for it.

---

*Heavenly Father, thank you that you are for me and for my marriage! I pray that you would strengthen our marriage and give us a vision for why you put the two of us together. Yes, to bring a picture of Christ and his Bride, the church, to the world, and yes, to show how much you, the Trinity, love each other. But is there any other reason as well, Lord? In the here and now, what do you have for us to do and to bring? For each*

*other, our family, our friends, our neighbors, our*
*world? I trust you to show us. In Jesus' name, amen.*

---

For Christ's love compels us.
(2 Corinthians 5:14)

# Opposites on Purpose

◦◦◦

*Be completely humble and gentle; be patient,*
*bearing with one another in love.*

—Ephesians 4:2

We bear the image of God; we are made in the image of love. We are created to love and be loved. And there is no greater context, no better opportunity to really love someone and be loved by that person throughout an entire lifetime than you will find in marriage. Of course, it is dangerous as well—the two always go together. There is no greater place for damage, too, because there is no greater place for glory. God uses marriage to bring us the possibility of the deepest joys in life; Satan tries to use it for destruction.

We are different from each other. God loves our uniqueness. The enemy will try to use our differences to separate us.

There is an old saying about married couples: if the two of you are the same, then one of you isn't necessary! Of course we are different from each other. We are given to each other to complete the other—to bring strength where one is weak, a way of seeing where one cannot see. In fact, character flaws are even gifts as well! Iron sharpens iron by rubbing against it. It doesn't feel too great for the iron, but being irritated by a spouse's annoying differences or habits provides us with the opportunity to seek the Holy Spirit's help to love through us in spite of our irritation!

When beginning a new project, you wouldn't hire two people with exactly the same skills when other skills are needed as well. You would hire one to fill a certain position and another for a different one. Yes, two are better than one. We *need* each other!

God wants us to enjoy each other's differences. Yes, sometimes the differences will drive us crazy, but more often, they can be a source of laughter and an inner surrender to the God who made the other person too.

---

*Thank you, God, for giving me my spouse. I pray for your grace to see our differences not as a bad thing but as a good thing. Please give me your eyes for my spouse. In Jesus' name, amen.*

---

Above all, love each other deeply, because love
covers over a multitude of sins. (1 Peter 4:8)

# *He Comes to Save*

∽

*For the Son of Man came to seek and to*
*save what was lost.*

—Luke 19:10

He comes to heal. He comes to save.

This is how Jesus describes his mission; this is how he sees it. Notice the choice of words: he says he came to seek and save "*what was lost.*" All that was lost (and oh, how much has been lost). Including all the beauty and power of a marriage. Marriage was *his* idea, after all. God created marriage and put the desire in our hearts. However else you think you came together, what other forces you think were at work, the hopeful truth is that marriage—including *your* marriage—is something God cares deeply about. When through the prophet Malachi (2:16), the Lord God of Israel says, "I hate divorce," we hear it with a shudder. But it ought to be with a surge of hope. The passion conveyed in those three words reveals how deeply he *loves* marriage, how strong are his vested interests in its success.

Therefore, we have all the resources of God's heart toward us and all the resources of his kingdom for the restoration of what was lost in our hearts, our lives, and our marriages. We have no idea how couples make it without God's help. Asking your marriage to flourish without God is like asking a tree to blossom without sunshine and water. Some sort of tree might grow, but you're not going to like the looks of it. The hope we offer is that the Christian gospel brings with it restoration and *life*.

Most of you have heard of the famous Cross, the assurance of forgiveness (and Lord knows we'll need buckets of that as we go along). In the cross, God undergoes utter forsakenness so that we will never be forsaken. He understands sorrow, pain, rejection, misunderstanding, abandonment. But what follows is for some reason less well known, or at least less understood—the *Resurrection,* the triumph of the life of God. This is as central to Christianity as the Cross, perhaps even more so. Because it is that *life* he offers to us. George MacDonald explains, "The whole history is a divine agony to give divine life to creatures. The outcome of that agony…will be radiant life, whereof joy unspeakable is the flower."

Letting that life into a marriage is the sunshine and water for the parched tree; it's like opening all the doors and windows of a house long boarded up. Light and fresh air pour in. It's like a rain shower in a thirsty desert. Everything bursts into bloom—the flower of joy unspeakable. The life of God brings resurrection—a return of real love, genuine companionship, romance, joy, long-suffering, and a shared mission.

---

*Dear God, thank you for coming to seek and to save me and to seek and to save our marriage. I invite your resurrected life into our marriage. I want all the love, companionship, romance, and joy and every good gift you have for us. Come and bring your life into us, and resurrect every lost and dead place. Grow our marriage into a beautiful masterpiece of your design. I know you would love to do that. So thank you that you will and you are already doing it. In Jesus' name, amen.*

---

How much more, having been reconciled, shall we be saved through his life! (Romans 5:10)

# *A Divine Disruption*

*I have come that they may have life, and have it to the full.*

—JOHN 10:10

When it comes to high-level expeditions, one piece of advice that veterans unanimously urge is this: Choose your tent mate carefully. For you are going to spend weeks to months on end shut in by foul weather in the forced intimacy of a tiny fabric cocoon with this person. By the time it's over, everything about the other person will drive you mad—the way he eats, the way he breathes, the way she hums show tunes or picks her nails. To keep yourselves from a Donner party ending, you must start with people you are utterly compatible with.

God does the opposite—he puts us with our opposite! Our mutual brokenness plays off of each other so perfectly it's frightening. It's like throwing a dog and a cat in a dryer together. Is he absolutely mad? Why would God do such a thing?

Because marriage is a divine conspiracy.

It is a conspiracy divinely arranged and with divine intent.

God lures us into marriage through love and sex, through loneliness, or simply through the fact that someone finally paid attention—all those reasons that you got married in the first place. The reason you came together doesn't really matter; he'll do whatever it takes. He lures us into marriage and then he uses it to *transform us.*

Consider fairy tales and stories you've heard. In so many of those stories, the boy and the girl each carry a fatal flaw. If they refuse their transformation—which is essential to the plot of the story—they'll never make it. Evil will win, they will lose heart and split up, and there will be no happily ever after. In the Chronicles of Narnia, for example, Shasta—given to feeling sorry for himself—is defensive. Aravis—holding a rather high view of herself—is dismissive. They are continually at odds, and the story cannot reach its climax until he stops grousing and she humbles herself. Beauty is a prima donna; the Beast has issues with anger management. She must find her courage, and he must find tenderness. In those stories, happily ever after waits upon a peculiar turn of events, at the center of which is the characters' transformation.

The fact that we all bring flaws to our relationships goes back to Adam and Eve. They fell, of course, and their sin is our sin; it has infected men and women ever since.

---

*Dearest God, I trust you. I believe you. I have been disrupted from my own plans and ideas in our marriage. Show me how that has been and continues to be you. I want to cooperate with you in your intentions for healing and life and joy in my life and in my marriage. Please help us become all that you have in mind. In Jesus' name, amen.*

---

Through love and faithfulness sin
is atoned for. (Proverbs 16:6)

## EXERCISE

How are you and your spouse different? Make a list. The longer, the better! Take a minute today to think about how God could be in each difference for his good purposes.

# The Journey

# *A Royal Mess*

*Create in me a pure heart, O God, and*
*renew a steadfast spirit within me.*

—PSALM 51:10

We are, all of us, whether we know it or not, utterly committed and deeply devoted to our style, our way, our approach to life. We have absolutely no intention of giving it up. Not even to love. So God creates an environment where we have to. It's called marriage. Take the fundamental differences of a man and a woman, add to these differences the fact that opposites attract and our peculiarities are nearly always at odds, toss in our profound brokenness, our sin, and our style of relating. It's the perfect storm.

Now listen carefully: God wants us to be happy. He really does. He simply knows that until we deal with our brokenness, our sin, and our style of relating, we aren't going to be happy. Nobody around us is going to be very happy, either. Most of what you've been experiencing in the time you've been together is God's attempt to get you to face your style of relating and repent of it.

This is the old Christian understanding of the world, the understanding that happiness is the fruit of other things, chief among them being our own holiness, and so we *must* undergo a transformation. Just as fairy tale characters must learn to move beyond their flaws, we must share in God's holiness before our story is finished. This awareness flies in the face of the more popular view of the world that's crept in recently—the happiness view. This is the idea that frames most people's expectations of marriage (and everything else). It's the view that we're here for our happiness and so you'd better make me happy. It comes as quite a disruption when we begin to realize that God might have other things in mind.

We described the first shock of marriage as that moment we discover it's hard and the second shock as that moment we realize both of us are royal messes. This is all actually quite hopeful, because these discoveries lead us to the secret of life—we are here to learn how to love. This is a love story, after all. And what does learning to love look like? Well, for one thing, it looks like compassion for our spouses' brokenness as we choose to turn from our own self-protective styles of relating.

---

*Dear God, thank you for your mercy. I am aware of my own brokenness…at least some of it. It's good to hear that actually we are, all of us, broken. And you came to heal. Your ways are not my ways. I sometimes think the goal is happiness. But you know that I won't really be happy without holiness, without healing. So I invite you to heal me. I ask you to heal my beloved. Thank you that you will and you are! In Jesus' name I pray, amen.*

His banner over me is love.
(Song of Songs 2:4)

# There's a Story There

∽

*Be merciful, just as your Father is merciful.*

—LUKE 6:36

Over the past several years, safe in the trusted confidants of our small group, six of us took turns sharing our story. We each had an evening to tell the story of our lives. Starting with our childhood, we spoke of memorable moments—the painful ones as well as the happy ones. We unfolded the pages of our lives. And even though each couple had been married more than two decades, husbands and wives heard new stories that profoundly impacted them. Countless "aha!" moments. Many tears. Much mercy.

It was a beautiful beginning of coming to know one another in a deeper, more substantive way. Pieces of the puzzle of each other's personalities began to fit into place. "Oh, that's why you hate to talk on the phone." "So is that why you feel so defensive to me?" "Now I get it." Understanding our spouses by understanding the unfolding stories of their lives is priceless. We can come alongside them and help them overcome difficulties so much more easily and more tenderly when we understand where they are coming from. When we begin to understand each other's brokenness, we'll find a great deal more compassion for what was previously simply driving us nuts.

Whether or not you are intimately acquainted with your spouse's past, we want to encourage you to set some hours aside to tell each other the story of your lives. Maybe go for a walk several evenings in a row. Or talk in your bedroom after the children have gone to bed. You will want hours. You will want to unplug the phone. You will want a box of tissues! Pray and ask God to fill the time, to help you remember what is important, and to help the one listening to really listen…between the lines.

---

*Heavenly Father, thank you for the privilege of loving my spouse. I pray that I would come to understand more deeply the story of my spouse's life so that I might have more mercy, compassion, and understanding. Please help us to grow in loving one another well. In Jesus' name I pray, amen.*

---

Everyone should be quick to listen,
[and] slow to speak. (James 1:19)

# *From Changing You to Changing Me*

⚜

*Why do you look at the speck of sawdust in your brother's eye and pay no attention to the plank in your own eye? How can you say to your brother, "Let me take the speck out of your eye," when all the time there is a plank in your own eye? You hypocrite, first take the plank out of your own eye, and then you will see clearly to remove the speck from your brother's eye.*

—MATTHEW 7:3–5

There are two kinds of people in this world—the clueless and the repentant. Those who are open to looking at their lives, and those who are not. Folks who know they need God to change them, and folks who are expecting everyone else to change. We have great hope for the first group. The second bunch *chooses* ignorance; the damage they are doing is almost unforgiveable.

This is why the "apply some principles" approach to marriage improvement doesn't work. So long as we choose to turn a blind eye to our condition as fallen men and women, and the unique style of relating we have forged out of our sin and brokenness, we will continue to do damage to our marriages. And add to our spouses' hopelessness that things will never change. We don't want to add cynicism and resignation to our marriages. We want our spouses to experience, *She is really changing!* and *He is really thinking about his impact on me!* Such thoughts inspire so much hope. They awaken so much desire. Something begins to stir in our hearts, *Wow, this could get good. I mean, we could really go places here!*

This happens when we make the shift from changing you to changing me.

It comes as we accept the plot of the story—that this is about our transformation, and that all the happiness we long for waits upon our willingness to be made holy. To learn to love.

---

*Dear God, I ask you to open my eyes to any styles of relating that I have that are self-serving, self-protective, unloving. I want to change. I invite you to change me. I choose to repent of every way that is keeping me from truly loving. Please help me shift my focus from chang-ing my spouse to letting you change me. For your glory and in Jesus' name I pray, amen.*

---

"A new command I give you: [Jesus said] Love one another. As I have loved you, so you must love one another." (John 13:34)

# Helping Your Mate

✒

*Two are better than one…*
*If one falls down, his friend can*
*help him up.*

—ECCLESIASTES 4:9–10

If two lie down together, they will keep warm" (Ecclesiastes 4:11). The picture is one of soldiers, who from time immemorial have lain down back to back at night in order to keep warm in the field. God gave us to each other because we need someone to watch our back. Someone to pick us up when we fall. How different would it be if we went to bed each night with the vision of two comrades lying down together in the midst of a glorious campaign? This is the reality, whether we see it or not. We need each other! And yes, we have other needs as well.

Every woman needs relationship. It is a deep desire that can never be completely filled. It is an ache in her soul designed to drive her to God. Men instinctively know the bottomless well is there and pull back. *I don't want to be engulfed by that. Besides, no matter how much I offer, it'll never be enough.* This is Eve's sorrow. She aches for intimacy, to be known and loved and *chosen.* And it also explains her deepest fear—abandonment.

Men face a different sort of emptiness. Men are forever frustrated in their ability to conquer life. That's the "sweat of your brow…thorns and thistles" thing in Genesis 3:18–19. A man aches for affirmation, for validation, to know that he has come through. This also explains his deepest fear—failure.

A husband and wife have a unique opportunity to speak affirmation and love into each other's lives. We can help our spouses by loving them and offering them grace, strength, mercy, understanding, and a safe place to share their hearts. Husbands can speak directly into their wives' needs by their words and acts of faithfulness and love. Wives can deeply encourage their husbands by communicating to them that they believe in them, that they respect them. Ultimately, we can point our spouses to the love of God.

---

*Dear God, again, today, right now, I choose my spouse.*
*I choose to love him (or her) and honor him and offer*
*him what he needs. Guide me today, Holy Spirit.*
*Direct me in how to love, what to say, when to remain*

*silent. I want you to use me to be the number-one person (right behind you!) in helping him become who he is meant to be and seeing how fabulous he is. Today. In Jesus' name, amen.*

---

The Lord is my helper; I will not be afraid.
(Hebrews 13:6)

# You're Not Alone

*There is only one Being Who can satisfy the last aching abyss of the human heart, and that is the Lord Jesus Christ.*

—OSWALD CHAMBERS,
*My Utmost for His Highest*

We can feel responsible for our spouses' happiness and for their unhappiness. We think, *I'm not doing enough. I'm not enough. If I were a better man, a better woman, she or he would be happy. It must be me.* Let this go on for a while and we move from guilt to resentment. How you are doing becomes my report card. If you are not happy, I must not be doing it right, doing enough.

The good news is, of course, you're not enough. You never, ever will be. Of course you can't make each other happy. This should come as a tremendous relief, actually. And it's not just you.

It's everyone. Knowing this allows you to take the report card away from your spouse. How your spouse is doing is not a verdict on your ability to fulfill his or her life.

Let that sink in for a moment—how your spouse is doing is not your report card.

If your spouse is unhappy, his or her unhappiness—and yours—is caused by a famished craving we all have within us that only God can meet. As this begins to come clear to you, it will be an enormous relief that you cannot possibly make your spouse happy. Sometimes, yes! But not always, not deeply, not in a way that lasts.

You need some place you can turn. For comfort. For understanding. For the healing of your brokenness. For love. To offer life, you must have life. And you can only get this from God. Trying to sort your way through marriage without God in your life is like trying to be gracious when you are utterly sleep-deprived. Each one of us needs a growing relationship with Jesus Christ. A tangible way to love our spouses is to encourage them to spend time in the Word. Spend time in prayer. Seek God. He alone is the source of true life and happiness.

*Dear Jesus, I say along with King David, "My soul finds rest in God alone." I want my spouse to be happy. And I want to be happy. Thank you for knowing that and for providing a way for us. You are the way. You*

*are the truth. You are the life. Come and fill us today*
*with your love and your life. Comfort me today, Jesus,*
*as well. How I need you. And please come for my*
*spouse today, Jesus, as powerfully and intimately as only*
*you can. In your name I pray, amen.*

---

Never will I leave you; never will I forsake you.
(Hebrews 13:5)

## EXERCISE

Are there tender words of love that your spouse has spoken or written to you that you are finding hard to believe? Is it difficult at times to receive the love as true? Take some time to consider why that may be.

Is it because of an incongruity between your husband or wife's words and actions? (What he or she is doing is screaming so loudly that you can't hear what is being said?) Pray. Talk with God about this. Journal. When you sense the time is right, gently bring this up with your spouse.

Or is it because of some deep rooted belief in you, based on your own story, that you find it hard to believe you are worthy of being loved? God wants to come for you here. He has said—and says today—"I have chosen you. You are Mine. I have loved you with an everlasting love." Invite God into this place.

It is difficult to love well when we ourselves feel unworthy of being loved. It grieves our spouses when the love and affection they have for us bounces off our hearts like a rubber ball. Today, risk believing. Try it on.

# Companionship

# DAY 1

## *Beauty of the Foundation*

*Love and faithfulness meet together;*
*righteousness and peace kiss each other.*

—Psalm 85:10

In the early hours of this morning, I (John) was sitting here thinking, *What is it I've most enjoyed with Stasi? What is it I would say has been her greatest gift to me?* The question drew me to the real substance of our marriage—companionship. Don't get me wrong. I love passion, romance, and sexual intimacy. Eros is intoxicating. But eros does not a marriage make. The richest part, the *daily* goodness, is companionship. Who else is always there at the end of the day, every day? Who else is with me in the dark hours of the night? Who else is by my side in joy and in sorrow?

No one but your spouse even comes close to sharing your life. Being married is saying to your spouse, "I will be your witness.

I will be your companion. Through thick and thin, the good and the bad, in sickness and in health, we are in this thing together." Isn't this the essence of what God was expressing when he said, "It is not good for the man to be alone" (Genesis 2:18)? But of course. Passion comes and goes like thunderstorms. Romance blossoms like night-blooming flowers. Companionship is far more steady, more day in and day out, like the presence of God, who says "I am with you always." We promised that in our vows, didn't we? "I am here to stay."

It might not have the drama that sexual passion offers, but "How was your day?" might sum up the most beautiful gift a marriage offers.

---

*Dear Jesus, thank you for the gift of companionship in my marriage. I pray it would increase. I pray to offer to my spouse my attention, my presence. Help me take time today to really ask how she is doing and wait for and listen to her response. I long for my spouse to offer companionship to me, Jesus. I ask for that. But today, help me to offer it to her. In your name I pray, amen.*

---

Let love and faithfulness never leave you.
(Proverbs 3:3)

# DAY 2

# *Strengthening Your Relationship*

❧

*In his love and mercy he redeemed them.*

—Isaiah 63:9

Life wears us down. Life wears marriages down. Busyness. Trials. Relationships. Work. Children. Simply the pace at which we live. Left unchecked, we can wake one morning with our spouses and not have a clue as to who they are or why in the world they are sharing our bed! Too often, despite our vows, our hopes and dreams, most couples end up living separate lives.

John and I walked to the brink of divorce in our tenth year of marriage, when we were about as distant as two lives can get. We both looked over that precipice, and we didn't like what we saw. By the grace of God—and his grace is always what's behind a good marriage—we began to make choices to move toward one another. We began to pursue our own healing more deeply. And we began to pursue each other by *playing together.*

This can feel a little awkward if it's been awhile since the two of you spent time together. Initiate it anyway, and don't be put off if your first few efforts aren't warmly received. A friend tried to get her husband to enjoy bubble baths; *that* was a miss. Watching *American Idol* might be a miss. Bass fishing might be a miss. But you are going to have to find some meeting place. Tennis. Beach-combing. Vietnamese food. A favorite TV show. Scrabble. Square dancing. Maybe it's just best to ask your spouse what he or she would like to do and do that!

Our marriages need to be nourished by time spent together playing, laughing, talking. It helps us remember what drew us to each other in the first place and discover new good things about each other. Plus, it adds to the shared history of our lives and knits our days and our hearts together.

---

*Dear God, there doesn't seem to be enough time in my day to get done everything that needs doing. I often feel like I'm failing at "doing life." And now I need to be playing with my spouse too? I get it. I enjoy laughing and times of just resting together. Walking. Enjoying a sunset. But I am going to need your help to shift my focus and make that a priority and a reality. Please help us build this into our marriage and to make time for each other. Help us, God to do that this week. In Jesus' name, amen.*

---

Freely you have received, freely give.
(Matthew 10:8)

# Ebbs and Flows

*[There is] a time to weep and a time
to laugh, a time to mourn and a time
to dance.*

—ECCLESIASTES 3:4

There are seasons to every aspect of life: childhood, friendships, weather. There are seasons when we feel close to our spouses and seasons when we do not. Don't lose heart. Ebbs and flows are part of the natural rhythm of life. They serve a purpose. When we are lonely, it drives us to deepen our relationships with others and with God. Droughts cause roots to go deep. No one is happy all the time.

A perfect life—always happy, flowing with ease—is not a reality. And by the way, there is no such thing as the perfect spouse either; that's the stuff of *The Stepford Wives* fantasy weirdness. The best husband for you is the husband you have; the best wife for you is the wife you have. Consider Nathalia Crane's lines in light of your present circumstances:

You cannot choose your battlefield
God does that for you;
But you can plant a standard
Where a standard never flew.
—("The Colors," *The Singing Crow and Other Poems,* 1926)

In other words, here you are. Make your stand. This is the man or woman whose heart you have been entrusted with. You really have no idea what depths of companionship are available until you venture into those waters and explore them for many years. Besides, your transformation is barely underway. Who knows all that God has in store for the both of you? We would say that after twenty-five years, we are just beginning to understand.

---

*Dear Father, thank you for my spouse. I love it when times are great between us and I don't like it when things are trying. But you are the Lord of all my life and every season. I pray that our roots would go deep into you. Please train us to turn to you to have our needs met…so that we might offer love to each other*

*when we feel like it and when we don't. Help us dis-*
*cover the companionship and the transformation that*
*is available to us. And make our marriage a beauty to*
*behold. In Jesus' precious name I pray, amen.*

---

God is love. Whoever lives in love lives in God,
and God in him. (1 John 4:16)

By the way, both of you need the camaraderie of friends outside the marriage as well! You want to be able to offer something to your spouse that comes from a full heart and not merely bring your need. Your friendships help you return home with something to give.

# DAY 4

# *Shared Mission*

*"And let them rule"…. God blessed them and
said to them, "Be fruitful."*

—Genesis 1:26, 28

Notice that when God blessed mankind with a mission in Genesis chapter 1, he gave it to the man and woman *together*. God is making something clear: *you are in this together*.

He then illustrates the point in chapter 2. Adam has just finished his first assignment as governor (naming the animals) when God interrupts to pronounce, "It is not good for the man to be alone. I will make a helper suitable for him" (Genesis 2:18). The fellow has just rolled up his sleeves when God calls a halt because something is missing; some*one* is missing. Enter Eve, Adam's companion. This is not about clean socks and pot roast on Fridays. God calls her Adam's *ezer knegdo,* a very powerful name indeed, only used of God in Scripture when his help is desperately needed. The woman is man's essential comrade, his lifesaver. And so the two are forever entwined—the couple and the mission, the mission and the couple.

The implications are pretty staggering—we have a mission we cannot fulfill without each other. We're in this together. That is God's gift to man and wife. The two of you are part of something beautiful and dangerous. This is crucial to a Christian understanding of marriage.

So what's the mission of your marriage? What are the two of you called to *together*? Can you name it? "We're in this together" is essential for the boy and girl in the fairy tale. Finding a shared mission as a couple is essential to a vibrant marriage. It might be the very thing to rescue a floundering couple, and it will surely take you both to a whole new level of companionship, regardless of where you are.

---

*Dear God, thank you that you have a higher purpose for our marriage than I even imagined. There are dreams you placed in both our hearts, with desires, hopes, visions. I pray you would rekindle those and help us to begin to dream together. What is it you have planted in us? What would we love to do? How are we to assist the invasion of your Kingdom into the realm*

*of this earth and bring your life and love? I look to you.*
*With hope and expectation and thanks! In Jesus' name,*
*amen.*

---

For this reason a man will leave his father and
mother and be united to his wife, and they will
become one flesh. (Genesis 2:24)

# Jesus—Your Closest Friend

*Greater love has no one than this, that he lay
down his life for his friends.... I have called
you friends.*

JOHN 15:13, 15

The greatest gift you can give to your marriage is a real relationship with Jesus Christ.

We're not talking about simply believing in God. There are many good people who believe in God, but for all practical purposes, they still look to their spouses to make them happy. Simply look at their anger, their confusion, their sorrow. We're talking about a relationship where you are finding in God the life and love your soul so desperately needs. This is not something reserved for mystical saints. The love of God is real and personal and available. He *wants* to be this for you. It is the reason he gave to each of us this famished craving and a leaky cup. To offer life, you have to have life.

*The secret of happiness is this: God is the love you are longing for.*

And let us all remember Thomas à Kempis: "Without a friend thou canst not well live; and if Jesus be not above all friends to thee, thou shalt be indeed sad and desolate." There is no friend like Jesus, and the most important thing in our lives is to find friendship with him. Wherever we are, he is always there, the truest and most faithful companion you could ever have.

---

*Dearest Jesus, thank you that you have called me friend. It is true. You are the best friend I could ever have or hope for. I pray that our friendship will deepen. I pray to know you more intimately, and truly. I pray you'd reveal yourself to me through your Word and through your creation. All I know about you is that you are marvelous. And I pray to know you even more and to draw my life from you. Help me to do that, Lord. I know you will. In Your name I pray, amen.*

---

A friend loves at all times.
(Proverbs 17:17)

## EXERCISE

Without telling your spouse, make one of these choices this week to put your spouse's desires and happiness over your own.

- Make a favorite dinner/dessert.
- Watch what your spouse wants on TV.
- Spend the evening or afternoon doing what he or she wants—whether that be cleaning out the garage, going for a walk, or a drive.
- Let your spouse pick the restaurant, the movie, the whatever, and let your response be a resounding "Great!"

Let this become an ongoing habit in your playing and in your loving of your mate.

# Your Spouse Is Not Your Enemy

# Set Within a Terrible War

*The LORD will march out like a mighty
man, like a warrior he will stir up his
zeal; with a shout he will raise the battle
cry and will triumph over his enemies.*

—ISAIAH 42:13

Think of all the great fairy tales—notice how often the kingdom
hangs in the balance; evil is advancing upon the land. What are
they trying to tell us? The very thing the Bible has been trying to
tell us.

You live in a love story set in the midst of a very real war.

The honeymoon of Adam and Eve—and their shared honeymoon with God—is barely underway when the evil one snakes in
with a plan to break everyone's heart. The devil convinces the two

newlyweds that they cannot trust the heart of God. He deceives them. They break the one command God gave. They reach; they fall. The beautiful kingdom is overthrown by darkness, into darkness. The circle of intimacy is broken.

The fall of man brought with it every form of sorrow and suffering. When Adam and Eve gave their hearts away in bondage to the enemy, they gave the world away as well. That is why Jesus refers to Satan as the "prince of this world." But our faithful God promised a rescue. He said, "I will come for you!" and the story of history tells of his pursuit unfolding, climaxing on a hill called Golgotha.

The battle for hearts continues. And it is as fierce as it could be. God gave us marriage, both as a picture of his love for the world to see and because we are going to need each other. We're not playing house—we're living in an epic love story set in the midst of a terrible war.

---

*Dear Heavenly Father, thank you for sending your only Son, Jesus, to save me. I take my place in his death, receiving his blood shed for me and your forgiveness. Thank you for his death and his resurrection! I receive his life! And thank you for the Ascension. I take my place in his ascension where you have given me, along with him, authority over every ruler, power, authority, and spiritual force of wickedness. I love you, God. I pray to wake up to the story that is unfolding all around me and to play my part. I pray for our marriage and all the life you intend for it. In Jesus' name, amen.*

---

The LORD is a warrior; the LORD is his name.
(Exodus 15:3)

# *There Is an Enemy*

❧

*Be self-controlled and alert. Your enemy the
devil prowls around like a roaring lion looking
for someone to devour. Resist him, standing firm
in the faith, because you know that your brothers
throughout the world are undergoing the same
kind of sufferings.*

—1 PETER 5:8–9

Peter is assuming that every single one of us ("your brothers throughout the world") are under assault by a very real enemy, whom he portrays as a ravenous lion, stalking us, just waiting for the first chance to devour. Not merely to tempt. Devour. If you've seen *The Ghost and the Darkness,* you have some idea. It was a sobering description Peter's readers would have *taken* soberly, living as they did in lion country. It might help us moderns to think of Satan as a terrorist—cunning, dangerous, obsessed—looking to destroy whatever he can in your life, with no regard for the rules of fair play.

We hear it, but we don't seem to hear it.

Most of us don't live as if our marriage has an enemy. When things are going terribly wrong, we blame each other, ourselves, or God. One of us may play a part. Maybe the whole part. But we are being dangerously naive when we ignore a key player in the story that God is telling. We are warned to stand firm against the devil, to resist him, to be on our guard against the accuser of the brethren. Satan is respected in the Bible as a very active threat, but few people actually *live* as if he is. Seriously—of the couples you know, how many recognize what Satan is doing in their lives and actually pray against it on a daily basis? Weekly? Monthly? When it comes to the enemy, we are all much too unaware.

You have an enemy. Your marriage has an enemy. Believe or not, this is very good news. You see, it isn't all you. It isn't all your spouse. And God is for you, not against you, for heaven's sake. Learning to turn and take a stand against the enemy gives you a powerful tool. Satan doesn't want you to take your authority in Christ over him because he knows it will work.

---

*Dear Jesus, please wake me up to the reality of the spiritual world I am living in. I take my place now in your authority and, in the name of Jesus Christ, command Satan and all his minions to leave me and my home and marriage, and I send them to your throne for judgment. Greater is he who is in me than he who is in the world. Teach me, Lord, to fight for our marriage and to obey your word. I choose to submit to you, God, and to resist the devil and command him to flee. In the victorious name of Jesus Christ, amen.*

---

They overcame him by the blood of the
Lamb and by the word of their testimony.
(Revelation 12:11)

# *Fighting For, NOT Fighting With*

∽

*Submit yourselves, then, to God. Resist the devil, and he will flee from you.*

—JAMES 4:7

Remember, God gave us the story of the first marriage to help us get our bearings. It provides some very essential categories for navigating *our* marriages—including how gender is so fundamental to our identity and how we were made for paradise. How mankind fell and what that Fall did to our lives *as* men and women. And it also makes something else absolutely and utterly clear: we have an enemy.

I mean, we all feel from time to time that we have an enemy, but the enemy feels like our spouses—right? Sometimes we just walk into the room and *see* them, and they feel like the enemy. "One day out of three," a friend cynically said to me.

Dear friends, if this is how you think, you will not understand your life, and you will surely not understand what is happening in your marriage. If this is not an assumption you use to interpret daily thoughts, emotions, and events, you'll be bamboozled! Pressed to choose our "top three things that would most help your marriage," we would come down to this list: *1) find life in God, 2) deal with your brokenness, and 3) learn to shut down the spiritual warfare that comes against your marriage.* Practice this and nothing else, and you will be *amazed* at the freedom, love, and joy that will begin to flow.

You have an enemy, and it is not your spouse. The sooner you come to terms with the fact, the better.

We live in a love story, set in a great and terrible war. If we will confront our battles for what they really are, against our *true* enemy, we can find our way back to the love story. It may take time and repeated bouts. Of course the war itself on earth will not cease until the White Rider returns. Meanwhile, our hearts are created for heroic love, and we will never feel more alive than when we are loving heroically.

---

*Dear Jesus, I love my spouse. I pray to be a warrior on my spouse's behalf. Please forgive me for the times that I*

*have believed my spouse is my enemy. He [or she] isn't.
I choose to fight for my spouse and for our marriage. I
pray the schemes of the enemy to destroy our marriage
would be exposed and defeated. I pray your resurrected
life into our marriage. Help us, Lord. We need you!
And you are more than enough. In Jesus' name, the
name above all names, I pray, amen.*

---

No, in all these things we are more than
conquerors through him who loved us.
(Romans 8:37)

DAY 4

# *Breaking Agreements*

*The thief comes only to steal and kill and
destroy; I have come that they may have life, and
have it to the full.*

—JOHN 10:10

Satan is a liar, "the father of lies" (John 8:44), so utterly convincing he deceived a glorious man and woman to betray God, whom they walked with every day. I think we tend to dismiss Adam and Eve as the idiots who got us all into this mess in the first place. But they had not yet sinned; they had experienced no wounding; they were man and woman in their glory. And they were deceived. It ought to give us all a healthy respect for what the enemy is capable of. Even the best of us can be taken in.

Now, what this father of lies does is put his "spin" on a situation. It typically comes as a thought or a feeling. *She doesn't really love you. He'll never change. She's always doing that.*

What Satan is hoping to secure from us is an agreement—that often very subtle but momentous shift in us that happens when we *believe* the spin, we *go with* the feeling, we *accept* as reality the deception he is presenting. (It always *feels* so true.) Once we buy into the lie, when we make the agreement, we come under the spell, under the influence of that interpretation of events. Then it pretty much plays itself out; it becomes self-fulfilling. These agreements begin to define the relationship. They certainly color the way we experience each other. It can be devastating to just let this stuff roll on unchecked and unchallenged.

The first thing we want to do is recognize what's happening as the enemy presents an agreement and give it no quarter. Fight it, resist it, send it packing to the outer reaches of hell. Recognize what is at stake here—the kingdom teeters on the hundred small choices we make every day.

Now, many of these agreements are already deeply rooted in our lives, some of them so historic and familiar we barely even recognize them. So—this will be an absolute epiphany—ask Jesus, "Lord, what are the agreements I have been making about my marriage? What are the agreements that I've been making about love? What are the agreements I've been making about my spouse?" To have Christ reveal those things to you will be absolutely mind-blowing.

As Christ reveals agreements to you, what you need to do is *break them*. You must renounce them. Here is a prayer you can pray right now!

*Jesus, forgive me for giving this a place in my heart. I reject this agreement. I renounce it. I break agreement with—[fill in the blank, what is it?]. I break this agreement, and I ask for your light, and I ask for your love to come into these very places. Shine your light here. Bring me back to what is true. Bring your love into this place, Lord. In Jesus' name I pray, amen.*

I have given you authority…to overcome
all the power of the enemy. (Luke 10:19)

## DAY 5

# *Praying Together*

*I tell you the truth, whatever you bind on earth
will be bound in heaven, and whatever you loose
on earth will be loosed in heaven. Again,
I tell you that if two of you on earth agree about
anything you ask for, it will be done for you by
my Father in heaven.*

—MATTHEW 18:18–19

One of the great secrets of the kingdom of God is the power of united prayer. This is all the more true if the two united are husband and wife. Remember: in the spiritual realm, you are seen as one. When husband and wife stand together, they wield a great deal of power and authority. The kingdom of darkness *shudders* when a husband and wife stand together in prayer.

The enemy knows this better than we, and that is why, whatever form his assault is taking, you will *not* feel like praying about it together. You'll suddenly feel irritated with each other. You'll bow in prayer, and suddenly you'll notice that he breathes heavily through his nose, and it will bug the livin' daylights out of you and completely take you out of the prayer time. Or one of you will want to simply "talk about it," which is not the same as praying about it; quite often this is a ruse of the enemy to prevent you from praying about it. Praying will feel hopeless; it will feel silly. Do it anyway. For if you will stand together in prayer, you *will* see results. You will have already won the first battle because you will have maintained a united front.

The Israelites had to fight to get to the promised land, and they had to fight to get in. Once there, they had to fight to clear it of enemies and then fight to keep it so. David had to fight to secure his throne, and he had to fight to keep it, too . God has long fought for the romance he desires with us, and he fights on even now. You needn't be afraid of the fight. The battle can be won, and it will call forth wonderful things from you, including courage and sacrifice, steadfastness and love.

We understand there are many marriages that feel more divided than they feel united right now. Your spouse might not be following Christ as you are; he or she may not be a believer at all. Do not despair. "For the unbelieving husband has been sanctified through his wife, and the unbelieving wife has been sanctified through her believing husband" (1 Corinthians 7:14). Your personal holiness and your walk with God have a powerful effect within your marriage. When it comes to prayer, you still have a great deal of authority.

Praying together is an intimate encounter; it will cultivate in your marriage intimacy and companionship, a sense of that you're in this together. Prayer brings us to a place of nakedness, and within marriage that is a beautiful thing. It might feel awkward, especially as you start out. Courage, friends; this is worth it.

---

*Dear Father, teach us to pray. Help us to carve out the time and to practice. Jesus, come and be the Lord of our marriage. Be the Lord of our home. I pray for your kingdom to come in our marriage and for your will— only yours—to be done. I love you. Thank you! In Jesus' name I pray, amen.*

---

If two lie down together, they will keep warm.
But how can one keep warm alone? Though one
may be overpowered, two can defend themselves.
(Ecclesiastes 4:12–13)

## EXERCISE

How do we learn to pray together? If we were just starting out, we'd pray together the "Daily Prayer" that we include in the appendix of our book *Love and War* (Doubleday, 2009, pages 213-17). Thirty days of that, and you will be amazed how much fog clears. We'd also recommend that you both read *Victory over the Darkness* and *The Bondage Breaker,* both by Neil T. Anderson. And listen to a series called *The Four Streams,* available through our ministry at RansomedHeart.com. These will get you going!

# The Little Foxes

# DAY 1

## *On the Alert*

*Catch for us the foxes, the little foxes
that ruin the vineyards, our vineyards
that are in bloom.*

—SONG OF SONGS 2:15

We all have an unwritten list of things that bug us. About life, about people, about our spouses. It's just true. If we let these irritations get under our skin, they can drive a very subtle, but very real wedge between us and our mates. We need to keep things in perspective. Keep a light heart. The socks on the floor and the empty milk carton in the fridge are not love-defining issues. Yes, we want to grow in awareness of each other and choose to *not* do the things that drive the other nuts, but we are human beings living in a fallen, messy world...and sometimes, well, it's just going to happen. Then what will we do? Love anyway.

Some things you will need to talk about. Pray for wisdom.

Timing is everything in the flying trapeze of marital communication. "How good is a timely word!" Proverbs 15:23 says. Along with carefully choosing our words, we have to learn *when* to speak them.

Are there certain subjects that always result in arguments for the two of you? Why is it that when you bring up the topic of money—or sex, his mother, her mother, your brother, how much time you spend at work, are you gaining weight, where will we spend the holidays—it all blows up in your face? It feels booby-trapped. Yes, exactly, it is. You just stumbled into the enemy's camp; you have just uncovered where he is working.

What will you do? Pray. Deal with it. Together. Remember: your spouse is on the same side as you, whether you feel like it or not!

Whatever else might be going on, you know God is using your marriage to make you holy. He is after your transformation. You also know that the log in your eye makes it hard to see anything clearly. So even if the primary cause for the crisis lies beyond you, it's best to start here.

---

*Dear God, I know that you are after my transformation. Why does it bug me so when my spouse _____. Does this interfere with my way of making life work? Does it rub against my style of relating? Is the issue really about my need to control or make a good impres-*

*sion or the fact that I don't like being pinned down?*
*Why are some of the little things such a big deal? Speak*
*to me, Father. I give you permission to change me,*
*transform me. I want to be a loving person. And help*
*me to love my spouse, to talk to her [or him] well when*
*the timing is right and to follow your lead. In Jesus'*
*name I pray, amen.*

---

Give all your worries and cares to God, for
he cares about you. (1 Peter 5:7, NLT)

# *Storms Will Come*

⌇

*Not only so, but we also rejoice in our sufferings,
because we know that suffering produces perseverance; perseverance, character; and character,
hope. And hope does not disappoint us, because
God has poured out his love into our hearts by
the Holy Spirit, whom he has given us.*

—ROMANS 5:3–5

Life is hard; sometimes unbearably so. Jesus understands this well. The Scriptures say, "Although he was a son, he learned obedience from what he suffered" (Hebrews 5:8). If *Jesus* needed to learn through suffering, well, it just doesn't leave any room for complaining, does it? How are we going to skip this class if he had to take it? Suffering will be a part of our education as God's children. This is NOT to say that every bad thing that comes your way is

God's discipline. It does not mean that marital crisis is some sort of retribution for past sins. That is bad theology, and it has hurt a lot of people.

We live in a broken world; disease, accident, and injury are just part of life east of Eden. This world has foul spirits in it, too; they cause a lot of havoc. The sin of man is also enough to sink any ship. Stir all these together, and you've got plenty of reason for suffering.

Having said that, we do have to accept the reality of Hebrews 5:8. Suffering is a mighty powerful teacher. There is nothing that will get your attention like pain. The good news is, it has a surprising effect upon us: it gives us hope (see Romans 5:3–5). Hope is a fruit of proven character; proven character is forged through persevering during times of suffering. Some hard times are simply for our good. There are certain things you never discover about God until you go through hard times; there are things you never discover about yourself, too.

These are hard times for marriage. Families are distant for most folks these days; community seems like a thing of the past; even church can feel less and less relevant (whether it's true or not). We're all so busy we have practically no time for genuine relationships— especially together, as a couple. And so we get isolated. And that is dangerous.

No marriage can make it on its own. We need the loving support of others. During calm seas and when storms arise.

*Dear Father, you know what is going on in our life right now. I invite you into it. I pray for your grace and mercy and love to overcome all sorrow and suffering. I pray to draw close to you at all times, difficult and not. Please give me wisdom today in how to live and how to help my spouse and me develop friendships with other believers who will come alongside us and our marriage. In Jesus' name I pray, amen.*

In all their distress he too was distressed.
(Isaiah 63:9)

# DAY 3

# *You Are Loved*

*I am my beloved's,*
*And his desire is for me.*

—SONG OF SOLOMON 7:10, NASB

The storms will come; that's a given. That's just a part of life. When they do come, you need someplace to stand; you need bedrock under your feet. When the winds blast and the waters rise—even if it's only *internally*—it is immensely helpful to return to some very basic truths. Truths you can stand on. The primary one is this:

You are loved. Deeply and truly loved.

Your creator says, "I have loved you with an everlasting love" (Jeremiah 31:3).

If all the pain of the world were gathered together and sorted by cause into great basins, the vast majority of tears would fill an ocean titled "Unloved." Because love is the deepest longing of the human heart—however hard we might try to pretend otherwise.

When things get painful in our marriages, the arrows that pierce our hearts carry some variation of this message: you are not loved. The arrows might be Rejection, Anger, Betrayal, or Blaming, or even Silence. But the message is, You are no longer loved; you never really have been. We've got to anchor our hearts in the one sure love. You are now, you always have been, and you will *forever be* loved. It might help to say that to yourself, every day. Maybe every hour. This is the boat that carries your heart right across that ocean of pain to the safe haven of God.

---

*Thank you, Father, for loving me. You chose me before the foundation of the world to be holy and blameless in your sight. Because of your great love for me, you sent your only Son to be my substitute and representative. You love me so much that you paid the highest price imaginable to gain me. And now, nothing can separate me from your love (see Romans 8:38–39). Nothing! Praise you, Father. Let your love go even deeper into my heart. I choose to believe you. I believe you love me! I love you, too. In Jesus' name I pray, amen.*

---

He will take great delight in you, he will quiet
you with his love, he will rejoice over you
with singing. (Zephaniah 3:17)

# *You Are Forgiven*

*He forgave us all our sins.*

—Colossians 2:13

It's probably safe to assume—since you are reading this—that you care about your marriage. (If you didn't care, you wouldn't be reading this devotional!) Okay then, it's also safe to assume that when things aren't going well in your marriage, you are sometimes prone to blame yourself. You are probably aware of all the ways you come up short in your marriage. What usually follows that awareness is that we start beating ourselves up. Yes, you have to own your part in the mess. But you bring that to the foot of the Cross, and you accept the forgiveness of Jesus Christ. Otherwise, your failures hang round your neck like great weights. All is forgiven. *You* are forgiven. This is the second great truth for us to stand on.

The cross of Jesus Christ was enough for all our failures and shortcomings. We are covered by the blood of Jesus! Cleansed.

Forgiven. Take a deep breath. Say this out loud: I am forgiven. Totally and completely forgiven.

Yes, we want to continually come to the mercy seat and receive forgiveness for our sins. But know that they have ALL been paid for. None of us is ever going to love or live perfectly. Only Jesus did that. And Jesus' blood covers us. Every shortcoming. Every failure. Every disappointment. Every moment we don't measure up. Every single thing. Jesus' blood is more than enough. For all of us.

---

*Dear Jesus, thank you for taking all my sins upon you at the Cross. Thank you that I am totally and completely forgiven. I rest in that. I have blown it already today, but you have covered that. Ah well! I'm sorry, and I drink in the truth that you are more than enough for me. You are my everything. Thank you for forgiving me, God. I receive it all! Now, please, live your life through me. Love through me. I need you! I pray with love and thanks and in Jesus' name! Amen.*

---

When you were dead in your sins and in the uncircumcision of your sinful nature, God made you alive with Christ. He forgave us all our sins, having canceled the written code, with its regulations, that was against us and that stood opposed to us; he took it away, nailing it to the cross. (Colossians 2:13–14)

# *You Are Secure*

*No one can snatch [you] out of my
hand…no one can snatch [you] out
of my Father's hand.*

—JOHN 10:28–29

When we married, we all gave a part of ourselves over to our spouses; we became one, in very deep and almost mystical ways. This is why widows and widowers often feel, *I've lost a part of me.* So when things get hard in our marriage, when there is pain and distance and we are clearly no longer one, we can feel as though our very soul is on the line. But we are in a safe place; we are in Christ. The third most important truth to always stand on is this fact:

You are secure. Utterly and completely secure.

You've got to silence the power of fear *right now.* Fear, anxiety, uncertainty, panic—they won't lead to one good thing. Not one. Quite often the fear is of the unknown future: *Will we make it?*

*What is going to happen to me? to the kids?* You are secure. God will not abandon you. Emotionally, financially, physically, you are going to be okay. Calm down.

When things get hard in a marriage, it can feel like the foundations of your life are giving way. Your mind races a lot; your emotions run wild. You begin to feel a little neurotic, like Woody Allen. It helps to keep reminding yourself of what is true—like Dorothy, clicking her heels together and repeating, "There's no place like home. There's no place like home." Say this out loud:

God is with me. He will never, ever abandon me. Not ever.

---

*Dearest Jesus, thank you that my name is written in the palm of your hand. Thank you that you have promised to never leave me and never abandon me. I rest in that truth. I am loved. I am forgiven. I am secure. In you. Please plant these truths deeply in my heart and may they be the firm foundation that I stand upon. Always. I belong to you. Today and forever. Thank you. In your name I pray, amen.*

---

Never will I leave you; never will I forsake you.
(Hebrews 13:5)

## EXERCISE

Take some time this week to consider what are your "taboo topics." And *why* are they taboo? Pray about them and invite Jesus into them. Spend a few minutes every day this week (or every day for the rest of your life) thinking about these truths: you are loved, you are forgiven, and you are secure. Type them up, and tape them on your bathroom mirror. Thank God, and choose to believe. Believing him will bring so much peace to your heart and so much pleasure to his.

# Increasing
# Intimacy

## DAY 1

# *Generosity of Spirit*

*A man's wisdom gives him patience;*
*it is to his glory to overlook an offense.*

—PROVERBS 19:11

When it comes to the transformation God is after, we are all somewhere on the road to redemption. Most of us are dragging our heels a bit, "creeping," like Shakespeare's schoolboy in *As You Like It,* "unwillingly to school." Sometimes it feels like our spouses have parked it on the side of the highway. And well they may have; you might need to talk about that. But even the best of us is far from the restoration we need, and we will drive each other nuts. Marriage is a submarine with Cinderella and Huck Finn shut inside. How do we keep from mutiny? from knifing each other?

Generosity of spirit. It is the single most disarming quality a marriage could ask for.

Yes, there are some things that need to be talked about. You needn't be afraid to bring them up—after you've asked God about it. But my goodness, if we stop to "process our issues" every time our spouse does something we find irritating, we'll never get past breakfast. (After you brush your teeth and spit in the sink, is it too much for you to rinse it out? Was that the last yogurt you just ate? You're humming again, sweetheart; I'd really appreciate it if you'd stop.) Most of this stuff you just let go. You simply let it go.

Remember, God gave you your spouse to help smooth your rough edges. God is immensely gracious, and he intends to make you so as well. Allowing room for your spouse to become who he or she is meant to become requires spaciousness—giving your spouse room to blow it. We simply choose to let their irritating nuances or thoughtless actions go. Rise above it; forgive before they even ask forgiveness; keep no record of wrongs; wipe the slate clean every day.

---

*Dear God, I remember that this is love and war. We are not just playing house. Please give us both a generosity of spirit so that we are gracious with each other. Help us to keep the little things little and not to lose perspective. I forgive my spouse right now for _____, and I ask your forgiveness as well. I pray to grow in love. Love through me and continue your good work of*

*healing and restoring both our hearts. Thank you that*
*you are doing that! In your Son's name, amen.*

---

Above all, love each other deeply, because love
covers over a multitude of sins. (1 Peter 4:8)

DAY 2

# *His Needs/Her Needs*

*We rejoice and delight in you; we will
praise your love more than wine.*

—SONG OF SONGS 1:4

Husbands and wives need each other. This is true and good. But
we don't need each other the most. More than we need each other,
we need Jesus. And the good news is, when we turn to him, we
find that he has been waiting for us. He is right here. Right now.
Ready and willing and able to speak to our deepest needs, to heal
our hearts, and to bring us the love we are created for.

A woman *needs* to know that she is loved, that she is beautiful, that she will not be abandoned—these are the very questions
she must bring to God. Ladies, your marriage is not meant to be
the primary place you should look for intimacy! A man deeply
*needs* affirmation; he needs to know that he too is loved and that
he has what it takes. This he must bring to God. Guys, your mar-

riage better not be the primary place you look to for validation!

We need our Father. We need God.

God wants to be the love of our life. He wants to answer our hearts' deepest questions. We just need to ask him. Spend time in his Word. Ask him to open the eyes of our hearts that we might see him and hear him. The truth is, he has already answered our hearts' deepest questions and needs, but he wants to make this *personal* to us. Yes, God loves everyone. But he also loves *you*. Intimately. Passionately. Personally. Ask him today to tell you what he thinks of you. And then wait for him. The truth is, he can't wait to tell you.

---

*Dear Father, I know you love me. I know you love my spouse. I know you love everyone! I believe your Word. But Father, I desire a deeper intimacy with your Spirit. I pray that you would reveal to me today (and every day) your very real, personal, specific love for just me. What do you think of me, God? Really. I look to you, and I pray to hear what you have to say and only what you have to say. Lead me in the truth. And God, please help me believe what you say. In Jesus' name I pray, amen.*

---

I have called you by name; you are Mine!
(Isaiah 43:1, NASB)

# *Sexuality*

❧

*There are three things that are too
amazing for me,*
*    four that I do not understand:*
*the way of an eagle in the sky,*
*    the way of a snake on a rock,*
*the way of a ship on the high seas,*
*    and the way of a man with a
maiden.*

—PROVERBS 30:18–19

Marriage is the sanctuary God created for sex, and only there, in the refuge of covenantal love, will you find sex at its best. For a life-time. The coming together of two bodies in the sensual fireworks of sex is meant to be a *consummating* act, the climactic event of two hearts and souls that have already been coming together outside the bedroom and can't wait to complete the intimacy as deeply as they possibly can. "I *want* you," says it all. The passion comes from the soul; the opening movements of this symphony take place well before there are four bare legs in bed.

God created the human form and the human heart to experience passion and ecstasy when we are fully loving each other—transcendent, earthy, tempestuous. It is a gift he intended us to enjoy. Often. This ought to change your view of God—he is intense about pleasure. It comes as a surprise to folks unfamiliar with the Bible how much God talks about sex and with such, shall we say, *enthusiasm*. At the center of the Song of Songs, God says, "Drink your fill, O lovers."

The sexual act is a stunning picture of what a man and woman essentially offer one another in every aspect of life. It is a metaphor, a passion play about what it means to be masculine and feminine. Many things go into a good marriage, but at the core is essentially strength and beauty. This goes way beyond sex. It is a reality that permeates every aspect of our lives as men and women.

---

*Dear God, thank you for the gift of sexuality. I give mine to you, I give my spouse's to you, and I pray that you would cleanse us, heal us, and restore us here. I pray that our intimacy will be a place of deepening joy and satisfaction and safety. Help us to love each other here and to receive every good gift you have for us. In Jesus' name, amen.*

---

Drink your fill, O lovers.
(Song of Songs 5:1)

# Offering and Inviting Intimacy

*The man and his wife were both naked,*
*and they felt no shame.*

—GENESIS 2:25

We live in a love story set in the midst of a terrible war. So it should not come as a surprise that our sexuality is often a place of disappointment, sorrow, and loss. Maybe *the* place. The enemy specializes in wreaking havoc with human sexuality; when he wounds men or women here, he wounds them about as deeply as they can be wounded. So don't be surprised when your sexual intimacy is opposed; the sanctity of the marriage bed is a war zone. Because we are broken people, often with very broken pasts, it can be hard to find consistent, abandoned, sexual joy in marriage. But much can be recovered, much can be healed.

And it is worth fighting for.

How do you recover the sexuality of Eden? It begins by offering strength and beauty outside the bedroom. The way you live and love in the everyday clears the path to your sexual bower, prepares your heart and heals your love for one another so that you suddenly find yourself craving your spouse.

The next step can feel enormous—talk about it. Talking about it disarms speculation, the playground of the enemy. It also requires you to sort through your own feelings about your sexuality, which is a very good thing to do. Neglect leaves room for the spiders and cobwebs to move in. Your heart needs to be fully engaged here; if it's not, you want to know why not. Then *pray* about it. Invite Christ into your sexuality, into your marriage bed.

There is an abandon being described in Genesis between Adam and Eve, a freedom with their bodies, with each other's body, with their sexuality and their selves. What if we could get back to that?! Jesus said, "The Son of Man came to seek and to save what was lost." The hopefulness of this promise is like a sunrise. God is about restoring the very things we care about too. What a relief. We've got big help on our side. He knows something about resurrection.

---

*Dear God, thank you for the gift of sexual intimacy with my spouse. I invite you to our marriage bed. I pray that we would have all the shared intimacy and pleasure and freedom that you desire for us. I pray that we would grow in offering each other strength and beauty every day and build into our marriage trust, companionship, intimacy, and desire for each other. Help us not be afraid here but have all the healing and life you created us for. In Jesus' name, amen.*

---

Be imitators of God, therefore, as dearly loved children and live a life of love, just as Christ loved us and gave himself up for us as a fragrant offering and sacrifice to God. (Ephesians 5:1–2)

(There are many reasons for sexual difficulties, some far more serious than others. Treat this for the beautiful treasure it is; take it seriously. The help we offer in the book *Love and War* will take you a long way toward the recovery of deep, mutual sexual pleasure. But the things we speak to in this book may not be the reasons for your sexual struggles, and even if they are, understanding is not the same as healing; clarity doesn't always bring restoration. You might need professional help. Love your spouse enough to get it.)

DAY 5

# The Reward—
# Deepening Love

*See! The winter is past;*
  *the rains are over and gone.*
*Flowers appear on the earth;*
  *the season of singing has come....*
*Arise, come, my darling;*
  *my beautiful one, come with me.*

—SONG OF SONGS 2:11–13

Isn't love the greatest joy of human existence? And the loss of love our greatest sorrow? Do not the two great commands confirm this? "Love the Lord your God with all your heart...Love your neighbor as yourself" (Luke 10:27). Love, for this is your destiny. Love God, and love each other. The banners that fly over God's kingdom are the banners of love. It's not about Bible study and faithful church attendance, not even dutiful marriage. Take the heart out of all that, and it will absolutely kill you. This story is meant to be a passionate love affair.

With God first. And yes, with each other. Your marriage is extraordinarily important.

In choosing marriage, you have chosen an assignment at the front lines in this dangerous battle for the human heart. You will face hardship, you will face suffering, you will face opposition, and you will face a lie. The scariest thing a woman can ever offer is to believe that she is worth pursuing, to open her heart up to pursuit, to continue to open up her heart and offer the beauty she holds inside, all the while fearing it will not be enough. The scariest thing a man ever chooses is to offer his strength without knowing how things will turn out. To take the risk of playing the man before the outcome is decided. To offer his heart of strength while fearing it will not be enough.

A lie is going to come to both of you in subtle and not-so-subtle ways. It probably has come many times, sounding something like, "It can't be done…it's too hard…we had unrealistic expectations…it isn't worth it." The lie to you, the wife, will be, "You are nothing more than a disappointment." And the lie to you, the husband, will be, "You are not really man enough for this." And so, I have two words for you today. Words that I want you to keep close in your hearts as you go forward: you are. Woman of God, you are radiant, you shimmer, you shine, you are a treasure of a woman, a gem—you are. Man of God, you are a man, you are strong, and you are valiant. You have what it takes. Hold this close to your hearts today. And every day. It can be done. And it is worth it.

---

*Dear God, thank you for my spouse. I choose to believe you today that I am. I am enough. Woman enough (or man enough). And I am the perfect mate for my spouse. I choose to risk offering love to my beloved. Love is the point. Love is the story. Love is central. You are love. Live and love through me today, Father. Give me eyes to see myself as you do. And please give me eyes to see my spouse the way you do. In Jesus' name, amen.*

---

Dear children, let us not love with
words or tongue but with actions and
in truth. (1 John 3:18)

## Exercise

Take a minute today to think of something positive you experienced as a couple in the last few days. When you have time with your spouse later, share that experience and talk about how it made you feel. If you have been married for many years, think back together and remember treasured times you shared. Thank God for them.

# The Most Excellent Way

# DAY 1

# *Healing*

❧

*Forget the former things; do not dwell on the past. See, I am doing a new thing! Now it springs up; do you not perceive it? I am making a way in the desert and streams in the wasteland.*

—ISAIAH 43:18–19

You just don't get through this broken, fallen, war-torn world without doing damage. A lot of the damage you don't even *know* you've done because it's coming from your own unconsidered style of relating. The cumulative effect of your sin and brokenness, the cumulative effect of your approach to life over decades, dear friends, has an effect on those around you. It's an effect you probably need to ask forgiveness for.

I (John) was asking Jesus the other day, "What do our readers need, Lord? What do their marriages need?" He said, *Healing.* So I asked, "How is the healing going to come?" And he said, *Forgiveness.* If there's to be an awakening of hope and desire, if there's to be some new frontiers in your relationship where you can talk about difficult things or handle conflict differently or approach sex differently, it is going to come through forgiveness.

Calm down. Take a deep breath. We know talking about this, going here, sounds like a root canal without Novocaine, but God is with you. You are loved. You are forgiven. You are secure. You just have a little making up to do.

---

*Dear God, would you please show me my style of relating and the damage that it has done to my spouse and those closest to me? I pray for healing in my marriage. I know where my mate has hurt me—even though he (or she) may not. But I am not aware of all the ways I have been doing damage to our marriage. I ask you to gently, kindly show me that I would repent. Deeply and truly. I want all the healing available, Father, and I ask for it—and for courage—in the name of Jesus Christ. Amen.*

---

By his wounds you have been healed.
(1 Peter 2:24)

# DAY 2

## *Forgiveness*

*He brought me out into a spacious place;*
*he rescued me because he delighted in*
*me.*

—PSALM 18:19

It will be the dawning of a new day and a very healing moment as we begin to ask forgiveness of one another. Simply to sit down together and say, "I know what I need to ask forgiveness for" (if you do), or simply to ask, "What's it like to live with me? What has the effect of my style of relating been on you over the years? Has it caused you to lose hope in certain areas of our life? I really want to know, and I really need your forgiveness." That would be so extraordinarily healing.

Now we know, we know—this sounds like jumping out of an airplane. Something in you is shouting, *Are you crazy?* We understand the fear. But dear friends, you can't ignore this. Eventually the buildup of all those offenses great and small shuts the marriage down because our *hearts* shut down—part of us, anyway, shuts down, checks out, catches a bus out of town. *It's never going to change, and he doesn't seem all that concerned about his effect on me. I'm just not going to desire anymore, not going to have any hope.* You don't want your spouse coming to that conclusion. So you can't just blast past your impact on your spouse and hope for good things ahead.

You know your intimacy with God is hurt by your sin, your indifference, your unbelief, your habits and addictions. In order to draw near to him, in order to recover the relationship, you have to say, "I'm sorry. Forgive me. I want to be close again, Lord Jesus. Come near to me. Forgive me for that outburst, for that indulgence, for ignoring you for weeks." This is essential to the spiritual life. And you also know it's not a one-time thing. Our love with God is nurtured by forgiveness, healed by forgiveness, recovered through forgiveness over and over and over again.

Your spiritual life can't go anywhere without forgiveness. Neither can your marriage.

---

*Dear God, I pray you would set aside a time for my spouse and I to really talk. I pray you would give me the words to speak and give my spouse the heart to hear me. I pray for wisdom and timing and grace. Mostly I pray for love. I have failed my spouse. But that doesn't mean I am a failure. I want to grow in love. I pray you would help us forgive each other and move toward each other. In love. I pray with hope, in the name of Jesus. Amen.*

---

Forgive as the Lord forgave you.
(Colossians 3:13)

## DAY 3

# *Learning to Love*

⚮

*Love is patient, love is kind. It does not envy, it
does not boast, it is not proud. It is not rude, it is
not self-seeking, it is not easily angered, it keeps
no record of wrongs. Love does not delight in evil
but rejoices with the truth. It always protects,
always trusts, always hopes, always perseveres.*

—1 CORINTHIANS 13:4–7

I think we all look for love to come in dramatic ways. We know
love is powerful and beautiful, so how come it doesn't *feel* like it?
Love plays itself out in what seems like such unremarkable ways:
you pick up your socks, you ignore the snarky comment, you put
the toilet seat down. But this is exactly what makes it epic—the
fact that love plays itself out in a thousand little unseen choices.
That's what makes it so beautiful.

Sometimes it is simply a touch. I (John) was feeling a little "bristly" this morning, like a pine cone with something to be resentful about, though I didn't know what it was. I simply wasn't feeling all that loving or loveable. Now, Stasi loves a hug in the morning; I know it brightens her day to be touched lovingly first thing. But I didn't feel like offering that. I wasn't in full retreat mode, just bristly. Before she came into the kitchen, I turned my back to watch some deer out the window. All spines. Stasi came up from behind and lovingly touched me. What a beautiful choice on her part. The bristles fell away, like blowing on a dandelion.

So many of these decisions to love are "secret" decisions, in that our spouses don't see them; they are between each of us and God. *I'll run to the store. We can watch your show. Yes, you can dim the lights. No, I don't mind if you go out tonight. Would you like a little of my cookie?* We meet these moments every day. Unseen. Unheralded. Immeasurably valuable.

It is in the little choices we are making every day that love is being forged in our hearts, our marriages are becoming what we long for, and we are being transformed. It is in making them that we are learning to love.

*Dear Father, I get it. I am here to learn how to love. I pray to learn. I pray to be transformed into a loving person—one who is known as that. Help me to love and to choose for my spouse many times today. You will see it. Even when she (or he) doesn't. It'll be our little secret! I give you our marriage today. Make it beautiful, God. Please. In Jesus' wonderful name I pray, amen.*

---

Beloved, let us love one another.

(1 John 4:7, NASB)

# *Why?*

❧

*My soul finds rest in God alone.*

—PSALM 62:1

Why in heaven's name would anyone throw himself *wholeheartedly* into such a dangerous, costly, and uncertain enterprise as marriage? (For wholehearted is the only way to live and the only way love is really going to work; I do know that.)

My answer has changed over the years. Yes, this is the man I want to be; that is part of it. The integrity of living well is so restoring, so deeply satisfying to the soul, it's almost addicting. Yes, I take my vows seriously, even though I had no idea what I was saying when I first said them. But there's something deeper that calls to me, something richer I have tasted that compels me to let go of the life I keep rebuilding in order to learn how to love.

I want God.

Can you name a better reason? There is simply no other foun-tain of life; there is no other waterfall of joy. God is the bliss we seek. This is what the Scriptures are trying to get across to us. Everyone who has known God and written about it down through the ages agrees. But it is a truth you pay dearly to finally possess for yourself. "There is no other happiness than God," wrote Pascal, "and our-selves united to him." But boy oh boy, is there happiness once you have God. David tasted friendship with God—after trying every-thing else—and came to the conclusion that, "Your love is better than life" (Psalm 63:3). Better even than life. Meaning, "I would give up my life in a heartbeat in exchange for the love of God."

God wants you to know this to be true for yourself. To know *him* in this way.

The Christian life is like the chapel of San Vitale in Ravenna, Italy. On the outside, the place is not that impressive; it could pass for a library. But inside—it is absolutely breathtaking. Byzantine mosaics cover the walls, vaulted ceilings are inlaid with gold, there are arches upon arches and engraved marble floors. It's like stepping into another world, a fairy tale. I'm sure they built it with the car-penter from Nazareth in mind. On the outside, he's not exactly your American Idol. But inside—he is the most engaging person you will ever meet. He'll take your breath away.

_____

*Dear Father, I want you. So I choose to love. I know*
*that every time I choose to love, I take a step closer to*

*you. And I do want you. I want to know you like
David did. I want to taste for myself that you are good
and to never leave your banqueting table. Jesus, you are
beautiful. You are amazing. You are strong and good
and noble and brave and true. I pray to know you even
more. I choose you. Come, take my breath away. In
your name I pray, and I wait with expectancy. Amen.*

---

But seek first his kingdom and his righteousness,
and all these things will be given to you as well.
(Matthew 6:33)

# It Is Worth It!

◆

*Love never fails.*

—1 CORINTHIANS 13:8

A good marriage doesn't come easy. Falling in love is how God gives us a push in the right direction. But then we have to choose. And we are going to need a very compelling reason to lay down our lives, day after day, year after year. To make those thousand little choices, for the thousand-and-first little time. Something needs to *compel* us.

What could be more compelling than this? When we abandon ourselves to love, we find ourselves closer to the one who is always doing that himself. We find God.

And yes, it will cost us. Loving costs everything. Look at the Cross. But loving is *always* worth it. John and I have been married over twenty-five years now, and I can honestly tell you that it just gets better and better. I loved John with all my heart when I married him, but God has enlarged my heart as well as my love. It has cost me. It has cost John. It has cost you. It continues to. *But so does every great, priceless, beautiful treasure that is worth having.*

Remember, we live in a love story, set in the midst of war. Love is our destiny, and all hell is set against it. We wake each morning and find that we have to fight our way back to all that is true, fight off the thousand reasons to settle for less than the life we were created for. Our bodies awaken, but then our hearts and souls must awaken, too, so that we might play our part in the grand affair. And God has made our hearts in such a way that nothing awakens us quite like some great mission, which is ours alone to fulfill. You have a mission. Your spouse needs you. The kingdom of God needs your marriage. And God is on your side. It will be worth it.

---

*Dearest God, thank you for your love. Your love surrounds me, fills me, and defines me—when I feel it and when I don't. Thank you for my marriage. I pray to play my part well in the great story that you are telling. I pray to love my spouse well, and I pray for our marriage to be a refuge, a sanctuary, and a light to the world. I choose my spouse. I choose you. Thank you for choosing me. Oh, how I love you! In Jesus' name, the name above all names, I pray, amen.*

---

Now these three remain: faith, hope
and love. But the greatest of these is love.
(1 Corinthians 13:13)

## EXERCISE

Take some time to journal this week about what God has stirred in your heart through this devotional. What have been new thoughts? Where do you want to grow? What tangible steps can you take to move toward your spouse? Ask a trusted friend or pastor to be in prayer with you for your marriage, and make a date with your spouse to share what you are learning. Remember, you are loved. You are forgiven. You are secure. God is for you. It can be done. And it is worth it!